Poison

A Play by Bob Hescott

Series Editors: Steve Barlow and Steve Skidmore

Heinemann Educational Publishers
Halley Court, Jordan Hill, Oxford OX2 8EJ
A division of Harcourt Education Limited

Heinemann is a registered trademark of
Harcourt Education Limited

OXFORD MELBOURNE AUCKLAND
JOHANNESBURG BLANTYRE GABORONE
IBADAN PORTSMOUTH NH (USA) CHICAGO

First published 2003

07 06 05 04 03
10 9 8 7 6 5 4 3 2 1

British Library Cataloguing in Publication Data is available
from the British Library on request.

ISBN 0 435 21459 4

Illustrations by Andrew Skilleter
Cover design by Shireen Nathoo Design
Cover photo by Science Photo Library/Oscar Buriel
Designed and typeset by Artistix, Thame, Oxon
Printed and bound in Great Britain by Biddles Ltd

Tel: 01865 888058 www.heinemann.co.uk

Contents

Characters

Nick Evans
Nick is sixteen. He tries to be friendly and to please people.

Ros Baker
Ros is sixteen. She is angry most of the time, but doesn't know why.

Doug Evans
Doug is fourteen. He doesn't mix much, he just listens to his Walkman, alone.

Stella
Stella is sixteen. She was excluded from school for being drunk.

Vicky Baker
Vicky is fourteen. She is always going out, sometimes all night.

Nathan
Nathan is twenty. He knows the world and has been around.

A Beginning ...

Nick is sitting on a street bench in the early morning cold. Nathan hands him a hot drink.

NATHAN: Drink this, it'll warm you.

NICK: *(Shivering)* Thanks – where am I?

NATHAN: Green Street. Did you have much to drink last night?

NICK: I was loaded. *(He sips the tea)* Why?

NATHAN: If you get drunk and go to sleep on the pavement this time of the year, you might not wake up again.

NICK: I didn't mean to. Who are you?

NATHAN: My name's Nathan.

NICK: Mine's Nick. Is this your job, waking up drunks?

NATHAN: *(Smiling)* I'm a chef. I work late, so on my way home I wake up rough sleepers and give them a hot drink.

NICK: Why?

NATHAN: *(Suddenly serious)* So they don't die.

NICK: No, why do *you* do it?

NATHAN: *(Hesitates)* Because I used to be one of them.

NICK: A drunk?

NATHAN: Yes.

NICK: My dad's a drunk.

NATHAN: On the streets?

NICK: Not yet. He's good at finding places for us to doss.

NATHAN: B and Bs?

NICK: No, he gets off with women. *(Bitterly)* He's just got married again.

NATHAN: Is that all right with you?

NICK: *(Sighing)* It doesn't really bother me … except …

NATHAN: What?

NICK: The woman he's married has got two daughters. They don't like us being there – in their house.

NATHAN: *(He looks at his watch)* Look, I'd better get on with my round. Here …

(He gives Nick a piece of paper.)

NICK: What's this?

NATHAN: It's my phone number. If you get fed up waking up like this – give me a ring.

(Nathan exits. Nick looks at the paper, balls it to throw away, then uncreases it and puts it in his pocket.)

SCENE ONE

Ros' bedroom and the hallway outside. Ros stands at her doorway, trying to stop Nick coming into the room. Vicky is looking in the mirror. In the hallway, Doug listens to his Walkman. Seventies party music and laughter can be heard in the background.

NICK: *(Upset)* We're sisters and brothers now.

ROS: Don't be stupid! *(She tries to shut the door)*

NICK: *(Puts his foot in the way)* We are.

VICKY: *(To Ros)* What did he say?

(Nick pushes the door open and walks past Ros.)

NICK: But it's true, we're stepbrothers and sisters.

ROS: Never in a million years.

NICK: Maybe you don't like it.

ROS: I don't. *(Folds her arms)*

NICK: Well anyway – here we are, all living together. *(He sits on the bed)*

VICKY: We've just got to make the best of it.

ROS: You sound like her.

(Ros points down to where the sounds come from.)

VICKY: Well, she's our mum.

ROS: *(Turning away)* How could she do this to us?

NICK: My dad's pretty good at chatting up.

ROS: *(Angrily)* How can we share our house with you? We don't even know you …

NICK: I know, but …

ROS: And just because they marry …

VICKY: We end up as …

NICK: Brothers and sisters.

ROS: No way.

NICK: We don't have a *choice* in this, do we?

(Vicky turns back to the mirror and applies lipstick as she talks.)

VICKY: They get married and we don't count.

NICK: Right.

ROS: Vicky gets kicked out of her room.

NICK: And Doug and I move in. Sorry.

VICKY: *(Cheerily)* Not your fault.

NICK: How many times has your mum been married?

ROS: Don't be nosy.

VICKY: *(Bouncing down on the bed next to Nick)* This makes three times. And your dad?

NICK: Twice.

VICKY: Where's your mum?

NICK: Gone, years ago. Walked out.

VICKY: Same here.

ROS: *(Crossly)* Vicky …

VICKY: Let's get it all out into the open, Ros.

NICK: Did your dad go because of the … partying?

VICKY: The *drink*, you mean?

ROS: *(Bitterly)* The *poison*. Hark at them down there. Like two pigs in their own …

(Ros stamps her foot hard on the floor.)

Shut up down there! Shut up!

(There is an awkward pause.)

VICKY: *(Trying to change the subject)* Your brother's a quiet one, isn't he?

NICK: Doug? *(Nods toward the hallway)* He lives in his own world.

ROS: Then he's lucky. I wish I could.

VICKY: I've hardly seen him.

NICK: He just listens to his Walkman.

VICKY: What to?

NICK: The sea.

VICKY: Who are they?

NICK: *(Smiles)* No, not a band. The sea. You know, like the sky – only wet. He listens to the waves.

VICKY: Doesn't he like music?

NICK: Yes – but all his discs got stolen.

ROS: A break-in?

NICK: My dad. When he wants a drink, he'll sell anything.

ROS: *(Snorts)* I knew it …

VICKY: He could get some new discs.

NICK: What's the point?

ROS: No point at all. They don't care about us.

NICK: Their lives are a mess. We've got to make sure they don't mess us up as well.

ROS: *(Softly)* It's a poison, you know. Before I had a carpet, I could smell it coming up through the floorboards. The fumes, the smoke.

VICKY: That's why I get out. And I'm late.

(Vicky grabs a coat and starts to leave.)

ROS: *(Suddenly scared)* Where are you going?

VICKY: Out. Bye.

ROS: When will you be back?

(But Vicky has gone.)

NICK: Off to see her boyfriend?

ROS: *(Angry now)* Don't be nosy.

NICK: She'll be all right.

ROS: No, she won't. How can she be, with her downstairs as her mum.

NICK: Does she drink? Vicky, I mean?

ROS: I'm lucky. I can remember before Mum became a lush. I had a few years that were almost … normal. Vicky's never had that.

NICK: It's a shame.

ROS: It is. You see, Vicky knows Mum loves the bottle, and she knows Mum doesn't love her. So she's trying to turn herself into the thing Mum loves.

NICK: I don't follow.

(Ros sits down next to Nick)

ROS: Vicky's trying to be a gin and tonic, a shot of vodka, a snort of cocaine. She's trying to be a cheap thrill, because she thinks no one could love Vicky.

NICK: *(Hopefully)* Maybe she'll grow out of it.

ROS: Don't be stupid. That's not how it works. You know that, your dad's a drunk.

NICK: Yes.

ROS: Anyway, you're right. We've got to make the best of it.

NICK: Work out some rules.

ROS: Right. This is my room, my space.

NICK: *(He salutes)* Out of bounds.

ROS: You knock, and if I'm not here, you go away. If I want to let you in, I will.

NICK: The bathroom?

ROS: *(Pulling a face)* There's a lock on the door – use it.

NICK: I will.

ROS: And tell him. *(She points to the hallway)* I mean Doug.

NICK: Right.

ROS: They might call us brothers and sisters but you know we're not. We're strangers.

NICK: Okay. Strangers.

ROS: Is that everything?

NICK: Yes … except one thing.

ROS: What?

NICK: Ros. *(He can't meet her eye)* You couldn't … I mean could you?

ROS: Spit it out.

NICK: Could you lend me some money?

SCENE TWO

Three weeks later. Ros's bedroom. Vicky is in a drunken state. She is being held up by Nick.

DOUG: Is she all right?

ROS: She's not being sick in here.

(Ros grabs Vicky and bundles her out.)

DOUG: Nick …

NICK: What?

DOUG: You didn't get her drunk, did you?

NICK: No!

(Ros marches in.)

ROS: Right. *(To Nick)* Why's she in that state?

NICK: I don't know. I saw her outside The Crazy Horse.

ROS: She's fourteen. She shouldn't go to clubs.

NICK: This man was trying to get her into his car.

ROS: She's going to get herself killed.

NICK: I grabbed her and ran.

ROS: That bathroom's going to stink.

DOUG: I'll clean it.

ROS: *(Angrily)* She's not your sister.

DOUG: No – but we're all here together now.

NICK: A sort of a family. *(He tries to put his arms around Ros and Doug, but Ros shrugs him off)*

ROS: It's only been three weeks since you moved in. It takes longer with me to get cosy. So clear off – get out of my room.

NICK: Right, come on, Doug.

ROS: He can stay.

NICK: Why him?

DOUG: Nick …

NICK: I mean, you have him sitting in your room for hours. But I still get sent away when I knock.

ROS: He's all right. He's quiet. He doesn't ask for things.

NICK: Money? It's not my fault my dad keeps me short.

ROS: What d'you need money for?

NICK: I'm young.

ROS: We all are.

NICK: You're not.

DOUG: Nick …

NICK: You're like an old woman in this room full of dolls. Is that why you like Doug? Because he's only a pretend person? Because he's a doll? Safe. Something you can control?

ROS: It's your brother you're talking about as if he isn't here.

NICK: *(Shouting)* And I have to share a room with him and it's driving me nuts!

ROS: So why d'you worry if he's in with me?

NICK: Because it's not fair.

(Vicky appears, the worse for wear.)

VICKY: Sorry.

DOUG: I'll do the bathroom.

(Doug exits.)

VICKY: Where's he going?

ROS: He's clearing up your mess.

VICKY: *(She flops on the bed)* I'll do it – later.

ROS: Yeah! As if. What were you thinking of? You could have got yourself killed tonight.

VICKY: Don't start on me.

(Ros points at Nick.)

ROS: Did he get you drunk?

NICK: No.

VICKY: Him? *(She looks Nick up and down)* He's just a kid.

NICK: *(Miffed)* I'm two years older than you.

VICKY: I go out with men.

ROS: And they get you drunk.

VICKY: No, I do that.

NICK: Why?

VICKY: When I'm drinking, I'm not here. Not here in your room. Not here in my head. When I'm drunk, I'm not … locked up inside.

ROS: You'll end up like her.

VICKY: Instead of being like you?

ROS: *(Getting upset)* She's not going to ruin me.

VICKY: Ros, wake up. She already has. You live like a nun. You never smile. *(Suddenly gleeful)* You talk to your dolls.

ROS: *(Hurt)* Vicky!

VICKY: *(To Nick)* She does. She has names for them all.

ROS: *(To Nick)* I told you to get out.

(There is a knock at the door.)

ROS: Come in, Doug.

(Stella enters.)

STELLA: It's not Doug.

ROS: Who are you?

NICK: This is Stella, my friend, she helped me with Vicky.

STELLA: *(To Vicky)* Are you all right?

ROS: Yes, she is. But I'm not. Now move it, get out of my room.

STELLA: This is nicer than Nick's. Couldn't we all stay here? I've got a bottle of vodka. *(She lifts it out of her pocket)* We could party …

ROS: Oh no. Not here. I'm not having that in my room. If you want to party, go downstairs.

NICK: *(To Stella)* Come on. We're not wanted.

ROS: No, you're not. And give me back the money you owe me. If you can afford vodka, you can pay me back.

STELLA: We didn't buy this. We stole it out of my dad's drinks cabinet.

NICK: You should see it.

VICKY: I'd like to.

STELLA: All this crap from their holidays. Green bottles. Yellow bottles. They never drink it.

NICK: It's for show, like your dolls. Why don't you sell them, Ros? *(He picks up a doll)* A collection of Barbies like this – you could make a lot of money.

ROS: *(Grabbing the doll)* Leave my things alone – and get out!

(There is another knock at the door.)

What now?

(Doug appears.)

DOUG: I've finished.

ROS: Well, stay who's staying, and go who's going. But no drink in here.

NICK: Come on. Let's go to my room.

STELLA: Bye.

VICKY: I'm coming too.

ROS: Haven't you had enough?

(Nick, Stella and Vicky go out. Soon rock music can be heard.)

ROS: You staying?

DOUG: If I can?

ROS: You're like me. Hark at them. It's all around us. Madness.

(The music fades away.)

DOUG: You can, if you want.

ROS: Can what?

DOUG: You can if you want, you know.

ROS: What can I if I want?

DOUG: Talk to them. *(He points at the Barbies)* To the dolls.

ROS: Do I do that in front of you? I forget you're here sometimes.

DOUG: I don't mind. When did you get them?

ROS: Mum's second marriage. The dolls belonged to Jane, another one of our family. Moved in like you.

DOUG: A stepsister?

ROS: Vicky used to have nightmares, so Jane was put in with me. Only … I got on with her.

DOUG: Was she quiet, like me?

ROS: Not really, but it didn't matter then. You see, we were almost a normal family.

DOUG: *(Sadly)* I don't know what that's like.

ROS: Jane's dad didn't drink, so when Mum got smashed he'd take us out. But it got too much … they left.

DOUG: No one took me out, so I sort of went in.

ROS: What do you mean?

DOUG: I just listened to music … escaped that way.

ROS: Did you have a lot of discs?

DOUG: *(Sadly)* Over three hundred. Then one day I came home late …

ROS: *(Gently)* And they'd gone?

DOUG: Yeah. Only the sea was left. I didn't know I had it till it was the last one left.

ROS: I'm sorry.

DOUG: It's all right. *(Changing the subject)* Why didn't Jane want her dolls back?

ROS: She did, but I thought if I kept them she'd come back one day. *(Ros starts to cry)* Everything could be normal again.

DOUG: *(Hugging Ros, sadly)* No chance.

ROS: No.

SCENE THREE

Doug, Nick and Ros are sitting in Ros's room. Nick has a hangover and Doug is ignoring him. A front door slams.

NICK: Oh no, they're back. My head.

(Vicky and Stella burst into the room.)

STELLA: Guess what we've got.

VICKY: A man!

(Nathan enters the room. Ros follows him in.)

ROS: *(Glaring at Nathan)* Who's he?

NATHAN: Nathan. Hi, Nick.

NICK: What are you doing here?

NATHAN: You rang me last night, from a bar.

NICK: Oh no, I'm sorry. I do things like that.

NATHAN: When you're drunk?

ROS: Why did you ring him?

NICK: I don't remember.

NATHAN: You have blackouts, don't you?

ROS: What d'you want?

NATHAN: Is there somewhere we can do this alone, Nick?

ROS: Do what? You stay here, Nick. *(To Nathan)* What's your game, mister?

NATHAN: Can I talk, Nick?

NICK: About what?

NATHAN: I'll start, and if you want to talk to me alone, we can go for a cup of tea.

ROS: He's not going anywhere with you.

NATHAN: It's all right. You rang me last night and said you wanted help.

NICK: Did I? *(Scratches his head)*

NATHAN: You said you kept getting drunk and you didn't want to.

STELLA: *(Laughing)* He knows you all right!

NICK: I don't remember this.

NATHAN: Don't worry, that's usual amongst people like us.

ROS: *(Sarcastic)* Nutters?

NATHAN: Drunks. D'you think you're a drunk, Nick? You did last night.

NICK: I don't know.

NATHAN: Did you mean to get loaded last night?

NICK: No, I only went out for an hour. I don't know what happened.

NATHAN: *(Concerned)* Does it often happen?

NICK: No.

ROS: *(Butting in)* Yes!

DOUG: It does, Nick.

NICK: I mean, I like a good time.

VICKY: We all do.

NATHAN: Is it still a good time for you, Nick?

NICK: *(Pauses)* It *used* to be.

STELLA: *(Putting a hand on Nick's shoulder)* We have a great time.

NATHAN: Nick?

NICK: Not any more. Now mostly – I'm frightened.

(Stella drops her hand away and backs off slightly.)

NATHAN: Why?

NICK: Because I don't know when I'm going to get drunk. I don't know what I'm doing when I am drunk, and I can't remember what I've done after.

NATHAN: I know what that's like.

ROS: *(Sounding unsure)* You're another one, are you?

NATHAN: I'm another alcoholic. A recovering one.

VICKY: But Nick isn't an alcoholic! That's stupid. He's only a kid. I mean you have to be old and sleeping under a bridge to be one of them!

STELLA: I look after him when we go out. He asks me to.

NICK: *(Looking at Stella)* I say, 'Look after me tonight'.

STELLA: *(Smiling)* Yes.

NATHAN: We're sick with fear, aren't we? We have no power over it. It controls us. We want other people to look after us.

VICKY: But he's not old enough to be an alcoholic!

NATHAN: Some people are drunks from the first taste. You know there are teenage crackheads, don't you? You've got friends who are addicted to fags …

STELLA: But drink …

NATHAN: It's a powerful drug. Some of us can't cope with it.

ROS: Them downstairs. Mum.

DOUG: *(Curious)* Can you catch it off your mum and dad?

NATHAN: No. But your parents' drinking can hurt you.

STELLA: My parents don't drink.

NATHAN: Neither did mine. Not a drop. But it only took me four years from my first drink at fourteen, to end up in a detox unit at eighteen.

VICKY: But Nick isn't like you.

NATHAN: Good. I hope he isn't.

NICK: *(Worried)* But maybe I am.

ROS: We're all screwed up here, I know that.

NATHAN: That's probably true. If your folks downstairs are drunks. Even if you're not, you've been hurt.

VICKY: This is lame. *(To Stella)* Come on …

STELLA: Nick?

ROS: Where are you going?

VICKY: To London. My new man's taking us.

DOUG: *(To Nathan)* How d'you mean hurt?

NATHAN: Maybe you already know. But the important thing is you can get help too. The children of alcoholics can get help, even if they're not drunks themselves.

VICKY: *(Laughing)* Well, I'll come and see you when I've been to a few more parties.

NATHAN: No problem. You'll find our number all over the place, and at your doctor's.

STELLA: *(Snorts)* Doctor's!

NATHAN: It's an illness. D'you know that Nick? It's an illness. What you made last night was a sort of 999 call, and I'm your ambulance. D'you want to talk?

NICK: I don't know.

STELLA: Come *on*, Nick. *(Pulling at his arm)* We've got everything from my dad's cabinet this time. Even the Greek stuff.

VICKY: We've got a car as well!

STELLA: Ring him when you're older, Nick, after a few more parties.

NATHAN: You can, Nick. Is this the right time? Only you can tell.

NICK: *(Angry)* I don't know! I borrow. I steal. I'm frightened. It doesn't feel like a party any more.

STELLA: Are you coming?

DOUG: Nick …

NICK: I don't know.

VICKY: *(Fed up)* Come on, let's go.

(Vicky and Stella go.)

ROS: Vicky!

NICK: *(To Nathan)* What about Vicky? Shouldn't she stop drinking?

NATHAN: It has to be her choice. Only she can make it.

DOUG: What d'you choose, Nick?

(Nick thinks.)

ROS: Well, Nick?

NICK: I choose … I choose not to be frightened any more.

(Fade to blackout.)